Getting More Out of Mass

SOMETHING MORE FAITH SERIES

By Fr. John Muir

Mark Hart, Series Editor

Published by The Word Among Us Press
7115 Guilford Drive, Suite 100
Frederick, Maryland 21704

22 21 20 19 18   1 2 3 4 5

ISBN: 978-1-59325-327-1

Nihil Obstat: Rev. Michael L. Diskin
Assistant Chancellor
November 8, 2017

Imprimatur: +Most Rev. Thomas J. Olmsted
Bishop of Phoenix
November 8, 2017

Cover and text design by Suzanne Earl

Made and printed in the United States of America

Contents

Heavenly Treasure

By Mark Hart
Something More Series Editor

A man cleans out his attic and fills his car with junk to sell. Among the items is an old painting. As he tosses it into his trunk, he notices that a corner of the canvas has been scratched, revealing what looks like another painting. Imagine his surprise when an art dealer discovers that beneath a simple, dusty painting of a bowl of fruit is a stunning and priceless work of art.

I recall this story often, especially on Sundays. The Catholic Mass is quite possibly the greatest "hidden treasure" in all of history. Jesus Christ makes himself available upon an altar, in every conceivable language, in every corner of the world . . . humble, accessible, "consumable."

The Catholic Mass is a *liturgy*, which means it is "a public work done in the service of another." As much as we work to make it happen, *God is actually doing the work for us.* We set out the gifts and light the candles. We assign servers and lectors and decorate the church, but it's God who brings it all to life.

To fully comprehend the greatness of the Catholic Mass, it sometimes helps to break it down into smaller parts. Imagine yourself as a rock climber viewing a massive bluff. It is helpful to take a step back and have a plan. Where are the crags and crevices in which you can place your hand and feet? Is there a group leader you can trust to help you navigate this climb? How can you get your footing and continue to move toward the summit?

A Guide to Reach the Summit

Consider this book your rock-climbing manual and its author your seasoned guide. Fr. John Muir is not only a skilled writer and trusted friend; he is a passionate priest of God and talented evangelist. As you'll see on the pages that follow, Fr. Muir has a unique ability to make the mysterious known in easy-to-understand language.

The more deeply you engage in the Mass, the more God can fill you with a new perspective, a renewed hope, and a more abundant life. You'll find that the word of God is, indeed, *living and effective* (Hebrews 4:12), not outdated or stagnant. You will discover that the Eucharist is less about our consuming God than it is about God consuming us with his divine love and mercy. You will be reminded that the Mass is not a spectator sport but an invitation to get into the mission field that lies outside the church doors.

Stop and offer a prayer before turning this page, inviting the God of the universe to open your mind and heart to soul-stirring new realities about an age-old practice. Allow the Holy Spirit to illuminate you as you seek to dive ever deeper into the love of God. Ask the saints and angels to pray with you as you peel back the surface of the Mass to reveal a great "hidden" treasure—a treasure worth more than gold or silver, a treasure that offers you not earthly riches but heavenly glory.

How to Use This Booklet

Whether used individually or in a small group, each session of *Getting More Out of Mass* is designed to take less than an hour. If you are using it on your own, remember to begin and end each session with prayer. You might also want to find someone to talk to about what you've learned. If you are part of a small group, the following guidelines can help you have a successful, fruitful experience.

1. Establish a prayerful environment by taking the time to pray before beginning. Ask the Holy Spirit to be with your group. Pray, "Come, Holy Spirit" slowly several times. Allow for a few moments of silence. Then say a prayer together, like the Our Father, the Hail Mary, or the Glory Be.

2. Have one or two people read the Scripture passage aloud that appears at the beginning of each session.

3. Assume everyone has read the commentary beforehand. The group facilitator could ask everyone if this is the case. If not, you might ask one or two people to try to summarize the main points of the commentary, or say what most struck them from reading it.

4. Begin discussing the questions, being careful not to rush to the next question, especially if not everyone has spoken. Some people need more time to gather their thoughts. People who tend to be quiet may need a moment of silence before they feel free to express themselves.

5. If the discussion strays, try to bring it back to the questions or text. Any member of the group should feel free to gently steer the discussion to the next point.

6. When you are finished with the questions, the group facilitator should go over the "Before the Next Session" section and ask whether anyone has any questions about it. Encourage participants to follow the suggestions in these sections at Mass the following Sunday.

7. End with prayer. Perhaps someone could pray spontaneously, thanking God for the opportunity to gather together to pray and study God's word.

8. Make sure you know when and where you are gathering for the next session. Encourage participants to read the Scripture passage and commentary and reflect on the questions for the next session before the group gathers again. This will help them get the most out of each session.

For more suggestions for small groups, go online to wau.org/faithseries.

Mark 5:25, 27-30

[A woman afflicted with hemorrhages for twelve years] . . . had heard about Jesus and came up behind him in the crowd and touched his cloak. She said, "If I but touch his clothes, I shall be cured." Immediately her flow of blood dried up. She felt in her body that she was healed of her affliction. Jesus, aware at once that power had gone out from him, turned around in the crowd and asked, "Who has touched my clothes?"

Catechism of the Catholic Church, 1116

Sacraments are "powers that come forth" from the Body of Christ, which is ever-living and life-giving.

A late morning in early spring, not far from the Sea of Galilee. Jesus has responded to a string of requests for healing: a man with an unclean spirit, an official whose daughter is at the point of death. Cries for help come from every corner: "Jesus, help me! Heal me!" In the midst of the frenzied crowd, one sick woman does not feel worthy to ask Jesus for his time, but she has utter faith that drawing near to this miracle worker will make all the difference. She reaches out and touches his clothes. A mysterious power flows from his body to hers. She is healed.

Then an intriguing drama unfolds. Jesus asks who has touched his clothes. His disciples are bewildered. Who's keeping track of that? It's a mob! The disciples' response implies, "Just get out of this crowd. We can't worry about one person touching you! Keep moving!" But Jesus stops and searches for the source of such faith. He knows that "power had gone out of him" (Mark 5:30) to someone who trusted that it would. Someone who trusted everything about him.

When the woman realizes she's been healed and that Jesus wants to see her, she approaches him with "fear and trembling" and tells him "the whole truth" (Mark 5:33, 34). Jesus lovingly assures her that her faith has saved her; she is cured of her affliction (5:34).

Is this just another tale of a biblical miracle, the kind of thing we can't hope to see in our modern day and age? Or is it something else?

This woman's remarkable encounter is a beautiful image of how Catholics can and should experience the Mass. The story offers a valuable metaphor: Jesus is ready to love us and heal us, but we aren't always ready to receive him. The crowds, the disciples, and all those who were unaware that power flowed from Jesus (merely by virtue of his identity and presence) represent the way we often, unintentionally, experience the Mass. What do I mean?

Two things connect this story and a typical Mass-goer. First, many of us do seek Jesus because we believe that healing power comes forth from him. From the hillsides of Galilee to contemporary Ash Wednesday and Palm Sunday Masses in the church where I am pastor, Jesus attracts throngs of people. They want and need something. So they come. That's great!

But not everyone who comes to Jesus seems to experience his healing power. Why was the woman with the hemorrhage healed? Why do some members of our families love God and actively live their faith while others don't? Why do some drift from the Church while others have powerful conversions? What makes some people fervently attend daily Mass while others would see such a practice as a bothersome inconvenience?

> Jesus' life-giving work is at our fingertips.

It's not because the Lord lacks generosity. The Gospel of Luke says of Jesus, "Everyone in the crowd sought to touch him because power came forth from him and healed them all" (6:19). When his power comes forth, it always heals. So what's the difference in results? The difference lies in our capacity to receive.

Ever-Living, Life-Giving

If your cell phone isn't charging, it's safe to assume it's your charger, not the city's electrical grid, that's at fault. If Jesus is the source that fuels divine life, we need to check our chargers when something is lacking, instead of assuming the problem lies at the power source. When we are figuratively hemorrhaging—losing our peace, joy, hope, love, and sense of purpose—we need to open ourselves to receive the power of Jesus. That's how we will be healed and whole again.

But how do we do that? Isn't it enough to be a part of the crowd, expecting Jesus to throw out a wide net of healing? Let's look at this through a slightly different lens: let's imagine the woman with a hemorrhage as a Mass-goer. What makes her different from others around her?

First, her receptivity to Jesus required knowing who Jesus was and how to access his power. Before she experienced his power, she "had heard about Jesus" (Mark 5:27). She had some knowledge of his uniqueness. Second, she trusted him; she trusted that he could heal her. Third, she knew that his power was above the things of this earth and that she simply needed to participate, even remotely, in the power of his body: "If I but touch his clothes, I shall be cured" (5:28). Jesus highlighted the woman's knowledge and called it faith: "Daughter, your faith has saved you" (5:34). Faith allowed her to know him and to participate in the power of his life-giving work.

How amazing that the Church calls the seven sacraments (and in a particular way, the Eucharist, which is at the heart of the Mass) not simply "visible ceremonies" but "'powers that come forth' from the Body of Christ, which is ever-living and life-giving" (*Catechism of the Catholic Church*, 1116; cf. Luke 5:17; 6:19; 8:46).

Look at that again! Powers that come forth from the body of Christ. Ever-living. Life-giving. What would our experience of Mass be like if we were to take that teaching to heart?

Do you trust that Jesus wants you to personally receive the powers that flow from his body? Do you want to know how to be more receptive, to participate in the Holy Sacrifice of the Mass more effectively? If the answer to both is yes, read on.

The aim of these sessions is to help you trust in the power of Jesus at Mass, as the woman trusted him in that crowd. We'll explore the Order of the Mass and consider how to encounter Jesus' healing touch in various parts of the Mass.

In the liturgy of the Mass, we can reach out, touch Jesus, and feel his power as it enters and courses through our souls. His life-giving work is at our fingertips. So grab on! An intriguing drama is about to unfold.

Questions for Reflection and Discussion

1. Do you believe in miracles like the one of the woman with the hemorrhage? If so, do you think they still happen? Why or why not?

2. Some say that if we are feeling far from God, God is not the one who has moved. Do you agree? How has your "receptivity" to God ebbed or flowed over the years?

3. What are one or two things that might be limiting your openness to Jesus' healing power?

4. In what situations do you find yourself struggling to trust God? What has helped you in the past to trust in the Lord in difficult times?

5. Does Mass feel like a spectator sport to you, or an interactive activity? What in this session has affected your view of what the Mass is, and what you want it to be?

Before the Next Session . . .

How often do you come to Sunday Mass feeling distracted? Perhaps you are thinking about all you have to do when you get home, or you are exhausted just getting the family there on time.

Whatever your challenges, try to come to Mass with a peaceful spirit by preparing for it in advance. What could you do to make for a smoother transition from your day-to-day responsibilities to entering church for Sunday Mass? Perhaps you could lay out everyone's clothes the night before or have breakfast already made. Maybe you could leave your home a few minutes earlier so that you don't have to rush to beat the opening song.

Above all, raise your expectations. God wants power to flow to you in this hour of divine praise and worship. Be open and ready to receive all that he has for you!

TWO

How to Enter God's House

Deuteronomy 30:4

Though you may have been dispersed to the farthest corner of the heavens, even from there will the LORD, your God, gather you; even from there will he bring you back.

"No eating on the run—we have dinner as a family!"
"Time for bedtime prayers."
"Will you be home for Christmas? We'd love to have the whole family together!"

Loving parents are "gathering" parents. They bring the family together for everything from meals to prayers to important celebrations. God, the model for all, is the same kind of loving father, gathering his children for worship. He invites us, rounds us up from the farthest corners, and welcomes us—always—into his home.

We come to Mass with varying mind-sets. Some of us are there because we grew up going every week; it "just feels like the thing to do." Perhaps we're there not for ourselves but out of love for our spouse, or to set a good example for our children. Maybe we're there in desperation, praying for a beloved relative to be cured of cancer. But whatever the reason for going to Mass, you've been drawn by the call of a loving parent. And he wants to help you get the most out of your time with him.

The opening movements of the Mass may seem meaningless or routine, but every movement has a purpose. The closer we zoom in on the meanings, the better we can understand how God is at work. Let's look at the introductory rites and discover how they help us participate in (rather than just sit through) the Mass, the heart of God's home, the place where he longs to gather his children together.

- Upon entering the church, we bless ourselves with holy water. Have you ever wondered why? Many of us would say, "It's a habit!" We can make it more than that. As you touch the water to your forehead, remind yourself that you are God's beloved child. On the day you were baptized, you were born of "water and Spirit" (John 3:5). Now the same Spirit of God is inviting you to do what you were baptized to do: share in his life through worship.

- The entrance song or chant begins. This singing is meant to unite our individual voices in communal praise of God. Each of us is unique to the Lord, but he also wants to draw us together.

- The priest processes up the aisle toward the altar. As you look at the priest, remind yourself, "He is bringing Jesus to me." (The priest acts *in persona Christi* or "in the person of Christ." Priests are Christ's agents on earth, uniquely able to be conduits of his grace through the sacraments.)

- The priest begins with the Sign of the Cross, which the whole congregation joins in, and then offers a greeting (*"The Lord be with you"* or another option). This greeting is also a blessing. Imagine that, through this blessing, God is inviting you to spend time with him. It's as if he's saying, "Are you willing to trust me, here and now? To be available to me in this hour?"

> Having acknowledged our brokenness, we turn to God and praise him.

Where Have You Lacked Love?

The priest prays, *"Brothers and sisters, let us acknowledge our sins and so prepare ourselves to celebrate the sacred mysteries."* We can't imagine inviting friends for dinner and, after greeting them, saying, "Please call to mind the terrible things you've done to me." So why do we do this at Mass?

Something like this happened to Jesus. He entered a house for a dinner party. Simon, the host, did not greet Jesus with a kiss or wash his feet. But a woman who knew she was a sinner came to the table and wept for her sins at Jesus' feet. Jesus praised her repentance and her capacity for love; he chastised Simon's cold heart, evidenced by his lack of hospitality. "Her many sins have been forgiven; hence, she has shown *great love*" (Luke 7:47, emphasis added).

The Mass is a banquet of great love. Sin is a conscious rejection of the demands of love. Sin, then, is the only thing that can block divine love. Acknowledging our sins (acknowledging our lack of love for God and others) has the happy effect of breaking our hearts open, allowing us to love more fully, as did the sinful woman. Use the priest's invitation to consider relationships, situations, and events in which you've lacked love.

"Lord, have mercy. Kyrie, eleison." At first, this might seem like rote recitation, just "something we say every week." But think about it. Like the blind beggar Bartimaeus,

who shouted out that first Kyrie to Jesus (Mark 10:46-52), we ask Jesus for mercy because we want to be made whole again. Jesus heard Bartimaeus' cry and restored his sight. We, too, are blind beggars before the Lord. We want to think we have everything under control, but sin is like an addiction, a blindness to truth. "Everyone who commits sin is a slave of sin" (John 8:34).

God, however, doesn't shame us for our blindness. As soon as we cry out, the priest delivers a prayer of remarkable confidence in Jesus' mercy: *"May Almighty God have mercy on us, forgive us our sins, and bring us to everlasting life."* From poor sinners to beings worthy of eternal life: God is the master of the quick turnaround.

Your Intention for Mass

We don't wait long for that taste of everlasting life. We sing that ancient hymn of praise, the Gloria (except during Advent and Lent). Having acknowledged our brokenness, we turn to God and praise him. We set ourselves aside and bask in our heavenly destiny.

"Let us pray." It's time to collect our intentions in the "Collect" (CAH-*lect*). Having praised God for his own sake in the Gloria, we now boldly ask God for what we need.

At the gym I enjoy group classes. Sometimes the instructor says (usually when I'm about to give up during a grueling set of burpees), "Remember why you're here!" It reminds me of my motivation and helps me to focus. At Mass, when the priest says, "Let us pray," ask yourself, "Why am I here?"

What is *your* intention for this Mass? What do you need from God? What situations, relationships, disappointments, hopes, and sufferings are you carrying? Mentally collect them, hold them in your heart for a moment, and imagine handing them over to the Lord.

Now the priest silently gathers the prayers of the people. He speaks or sings the opening prayer. The *Amen* of the people means "So be it." Substitute your own words, whatever words help you to truly mean it: "Amen, . . . yes, God, I'm in on this," or "Amen, . . . I trust you, Lord."

Having gathered his scattered children, the Father, our loving parent, speaks.

Questions for Reflection and Discussion

1. What has been your attitude about Mass? Have you tended to see Mass as God, the loving parent, gathering his children together? Or do you think of it as something you must attend to gain God's favor?

2. Have you ever thought of the introductory rites of the Mass as their own separate, important portion of the Mass? If yes, what part of the opening is the most meaningful to you? If not, what in this session has shed new light on the opening of the Mass?

3. How do you usually react to the "rote" and "routine" opening parts of the Mass? Do you find them comforting?

Boring? Do you see any of those portions of the Mass differently now?

4. Do you tend to think of sin as a checklist of behaviors to avoid or as a failure to love? Talk about the differences between these two attitudes.

5. Do you usually come with an intention for Mass? How can that practice help you to receive more of what God wants to give you?

Before the Next Session . . .

As you settle into your pew this week, take a few moments to think of an intention you would like to lift up during Mass. Say a prayer that you will be able to stay focused. Be ready to sing as the first note is played and the priest processes up the aisle. Pay attention to all that is happening, and enter in as much as possible. Remember, God has gathered his children together!

Hebrews 4:12

Indeed, the word of God is living and effective, . . .
penetrating even between soul and spirit, . . . able to
discern reflections and thoughts of the heart.

Romans 10:8

The word is near you, / in your mouth and in your
heart.

"How was your day?"
"Looks like you've got something on your mind.
Want to talk?"
"Honey, I'm sorry I was so distracted this past week.
Please forgive me."

Loving families communicate on a regular basis.
Relationships grow as families spend time together
telling stories, joking, debating, laughing, confiding,
and dreaming. Sometimes we get snippy or misunderstand one another, and then we need to forgive. It's all
part of healthy communication, and it's all essential!

The same is true of our relationship with God. When
we spend time with him at Mass, he communicates with
us through the readings and the homily, and our relationship flourishes.

Just as the day-to-day quality of communication varies in families, it can also be uneven at Mass. Sometimes during the Liturgy of the Word, the Scripture passage is exactly what we need to hear. At other times, it feels random or foreign. Sometimes the preaching is inspiring and motivating, and at other times it sounds like a rambling monotone. How do we clear away the noise and *really* hear God's voice?

Speak, Lord, Your Servant Is Listening

If the liturgy is a real conversation, how should you handle your end of the interaction? It may help to follow the readings as they are proclaimed, in a printed or digital form. Make note of which book of the Bible is being proclaimed. Think about who is speaking in each reading and what point is being communicated.

Even better, read the Scripture passages prior to Mass. (This "previewing" is especially helpful for parents who may be in and out of Mass with a fussy baby or toddler.) You can even involve the whole family, explaining the Gospel reading to your children, for example, on the way to Mass.

Each week look for one thing in the readings that jumps out at you. Is it a word, an image, a phrase? The Bible is God's voice, communicated to us through human language—so pay attention to the language! At Mass we listen for ways in which the Scriptures reveal the story of God's covenant love, which is his invitation to loving union with him. This requires a leap of faith—believing that God really is speaking to us here and now. It also requires the conviction that God desires to draw us more deeply into his love through the day's proclamation of the Scriptures. Try to put this faith and conviction into action at Mass!

When you seek out words or images that manifest God's covenant love to you, you are doing exactly that.

What if the readings make no sense to you, or the sound system is malfunctioning, or you zone out? Maybe the readings even anger or frustrate you. (That's okay. Strong feelings indicate the presence of a relationship, and that's better than being luke-warm toward God!) Whatever your internal response, outwardly you respond, *"Thanks be to God."* That's your acknowledgement that God is present and speaking to you. Even when you've felt no takeaway from the readings, you can be thankful to have spent time listening to your Father's voice.

> Know that God wants to speak personally and beautifully to you. He *is* present.

There are built-in times of silence to reflect after each reading and after the homily. Their purpose is to help us grasp the word, much as Mary did when she kept the things she had heard "in her heart" (Luke 2:19, 51). Take advantage of these times. This period of silence is not the time to intellectualize about ideas. Simply, consciously, hold the word in your heart.

This is easier said than done (especially if you are at Mass with busy toddlers, or the church is too hot, or a noisy fan is blowing). And outward distractions aren't the only things keeping us from holding on to God's word—our own minds are places of busyness and noise! But the heart longs for God's silence. So in the silence after the Scriptures, know that God wants to speak personally and beautifully to you. He *is* present.

The Homily: "The Lord Spoke to Me"

The first Easter evening gives us an ideal model for a homily. The risen Jesus walks with the disciples on the road to Emmaus (Luke 24:13-25). "Were our hearts not burning within us while he spoke to us?" they ask after they recognize Jesus in the breaking of the bread.

You might say, "But my priest (or deacon) doesn't preach like Jesus!" True, but Jesus speaks through your priest. You've listened well when you can hear beyond the humanity of your priest and say, not "That was a good homily," but rather, "The Lord spoke to me today."

That's the purpose of every homily. Homilies are not meant to be entertainment, lectures, or religious exhortations. The homily is meant to open a dialogue between God and you. Good preachers stir a desire for God in the hearts of listeners. They help strengthen those desires by removing the fears and confusion that can block openness to the Lord.

God is a loving parent who wants a relationship with us. Just as parents delight in the voices of their children and coax and encourage their little ones in conversation, God teaches us how to respond to him. The Liturgy of the Word is one of his tools. All that happens is designed to help us experience this familial back-and-forth.

And now that God has set our hearts burning in the Liturgy of the Word, we are ready to see him in the breaking of the bread.

Questions for Reflection and Discussion

1. Have there been times in your life when you experienced God speaking to you? What did you experience, and how did it affect your relationship with God?

2. How often do you read and pray with Scripture? What role do you hope the Bible will play in your life in the future?

3. How often are you able to sit silently with the Lord? In what ways have periods of silence helped your relationship with God to grow or helped you to understand God's word?

4. How would you explain the difference between a class or lecture on the Bible and what happens in the Liturgy of the Word?

5. Can you think of a recent homily that touched you? When the priest or deacon preached, what were your feelings, thoughts, or desires?

Before the Next Session . . .

Pick a time this week before Sunday Mass to read the Mass readings. (You can find them online at usccb.org/bible.) Pray with them slowly and note anything that jumps out at you. Stay with that line or phrase, and ask the Lord to show you what he wants to communicate to you. Perhaps you can write down that word or image and pray it throughout the week. Let it sink deeply into your heart and mind.

When you are at Mass, make use of the silence after each reading. Consciously stay in God's presence, and pray that his word will make a difference in your life this week.

FOUR

How to Give Yourself to God

> **Romans 12:1**
> I urge you, therefore, . . . by the mercies of God, to offer your bodies as a living sacrifice, holy and pleasing to God, your spiritual worship.
>
> "Will you marry me?"
> "I'm yours, body and soul!"

Weddings offer a unique drama. The couple beam with happiness. Leaving behind their old way of life, they are ready to sail into uncharted waters. As they exchange their vows in the marriage rite, the bride gives herself to the groom and the groom gives himself to the bride—all the days of their lives.

The Liturgy of the Eucharist is also an exchange of persons. In this mysterious exchange, we give ourselves to God and he gives himself to us, just as he has promised. So let's look at how this drama unfolds.

The offertory hymn signals the beginning of the Liturgy of the Eucharist. Bread and wine are carried to the foot of the sanctuary by representatives from the assembly. These people represent *you*; they are carrying *your* gifts and sacrifices to the altar. The priest receives these gifts and prays, *"Blessed are you, Lord God of all creation, for through your goodness we have received this bread (or the wine) . . . we offer you."*

Why do we offer God the things we hunger and thirst for when he receives no benefit from them? It's precisely because God doesn't need what we offer to him. Everything we are and have is his extravagant gift to us. When we give the essential stuff of our existence to him, it signifies two things: thanks and trust. We are saying, *"Thank you for your goodness,"* and, *"I trust your goodness."*

When the bread and wine are placed in the hands of the priest, it's a good time to be specific about what you are offering to God for that Mass. You can pray, "Jesus, I offer you my . . . " If you're clinging to something in your life, are unduly attached to something, or if you're fearful about someone or something precious to you, offer that to God. Nothing is too small or trivial to be offered at the altar, to be transformed for his glory and our good.

The Altar Is My Cross

"Lift up your hearts." The priest's invitation clarifies that our sacrifice isn't made up of our stuff—*we* are the sacrifice. Our sacrifice is our heart, because God wants our love. Our response to the priest is a pledge of our love: *"We lift them up to the Lord."*

"Let us give thanks to the Lord our God." Deep, abiding gratitude is at the center of the Eucharist. In fact, the word *Eucharist* is rooted in the Greek word for "thanksgiving." We respond, *"It is right and just."*

But what if you're not feeling very grateful? Perhaps you honestly cannot bring yourself to thank God because you have lost a loved one, been desperately hurt, or lost hope. Take courage from God himself. He knows how you feel. Jesus is the model and the reason for the fact that our suffering has meaning. His whole earthly life was one of grateful praise to the Father for the Father's work (which is often hidden to us), up to, and especially through, his suffering. When we join our pain to Jesus' prayer of gratitude, our suffering is transformed.

"Holy, Holy, Holy, Lord God of hosts." At this point in the Mass, we can focus on the comforting (and astonishing) realization that we are not forgotten, that God is not distant or indifferent to us. We are surrounded, as the shepherds were on the first Christmas night, by a host of angels. God is unspeakably close and is about to act in the same way he did at creation and at the moment when Jesus was conceived: through the descent of the Holy Spirit. He's coming directly into our realm.

> Why does Jesus do such an extravagant thing for us? The answer is love.

This divine action re-presents another night as well—in the upper room, at the Passover supper with his apostles. Jesus took bread and wine and made himself present under those simple forms. The priest now speaks the words of Jesus from that night: *"This is my Body . . . this is . . . the Blood of the new and eternal covenant, which will be poured out for you."*

At Jesus' word (spoken by the priest, who is acting in the person of Christ), the bread and wine change. (The technical term for this is *transubstantiation*. The substance is transformed, though the appearance of bread and wine is not.) Bread and wine *become* the Body and Blood of Jesus. He is really and truly present under the appearances of things we eat and drink.

The priest solemnly holds the consecrated host and the chalice, as if to say to the kneeling people, "Here he is! We are looking upon a miracle!" In this moment, try to silently adore the Lord in his Eucharistic presence. Why does Jesus do such an extravagant thing for us, even when so many don't realize or believe it? The answer is in one word: love.

A Strength Like No Other

The consecrated host now rests on the altar and we pause to pray as the priest says (in Eucharistic Prayer III), *"May this sacrifice of our reconciliation, we pray, O Lord, advance the peace and salvation of all the world."* The love of Jesus is meant for the whole world, not just a select, "religious" few. Catholics believe that Jesus died not simply to save us from a broken existence but to inaugurate an entirely new world. The visionary in the Book of Revelation sees "a new heaven and a new earth" dawning (21:1). So we go big: we pray through the priest for the final perfection of everyone and everything! Jesus is all about outrageous goals.

"Be pleased to confirm in faith and charity your pilgrim Church on earth" (also from Eucharistic Prayer III). This point in the Mass is a marvelous time to call to mind the entire Church: the pope, bishops, clergy, the baptized (both dead and alive), and those far from God. Let the names and faces of your friends, family, and especially your enemies, occupy your mind and heart. Pray silently as the priest prays aloud.

We Are One Body

Now the priest performs the Great Elevation (he lifts the Eucharistic elements) and recites the Great Doxology (which means "words of praise"): *"Through him and with him and in him, O God, Almighty Father, in the unity of the Holy Spirit, all glory and honor is yours, for ever and ever."*

In essence, the priest is doing the unthinkable and the unexplainable: he is offering God to God. And he has helps you participate in this astounding offering. Your *Amen* at this point is your great "Let it be done!" It is your freely given yes to this re-presentation of the sacrifice on Calvary. When you sing or say "the great Amen," remember Jesus' words on the cross: "Father, into your hands, I commend my spirit" (Luke 23:46). Try to adopt those words as your own as you pray, "Father, I give myself to you, with Jesus on the cross, with the whole Church, with all who suffer, for the salvation of the world."

Because this gift is of infinite value, there is truly nothing left to give. As we'll see in the next session, the result of giving ourselves to God will be a new kind of peace.

Questions for Reflection and Discussion

1. How does God give himself to you during the Liturgy of the Eucharist? How do you give yourself to him?

2. How often do you thank the Lord for his Body and Blood in the Eucharist? How can you grow in gratitude even when you are suffering?

3. When did you first believe that the consecrated bread and wine are truly Jesus himself? How did that influence your desire to attend Mass? Or if you struggle with belief in the Real Presence of Jesus in the Eucharist, are your doubts rooted in intellectual wrangling? Lack of trust? Or something else?

4. Who do you pray for regularly at Mass? Who and what would you like to start praying for at Mass (including those who are deceased)? Consider writing down names and intentions and taking them with you to Mass.

5. What do you imagine the "new heaven and new earth" will be like? Why is this something we pray for at Mass?

Are you shocked that Jesus wants you to offer him your most basic needs: your projects, family life, friendships, leisure, study, finances, successes, and failures? If you are—good! It *is* shocking. The King of the universe wants the stuff into which you've poured your heart, soul, and sweat.

If you're not sure where to start, think about who or what gets your best energy (at work, at home, on the weekends). At Mass this week, try to consciously offer those people and things to the Lord. Continue to make this offering throughout the week. Ask the Lord to give you the grace to surrender these situations, as well as your whole self, to him.

John 15:5, 9

"Whoever remains in me and I in him will bear much fruit.... As the Father loves me, so I also love you. Remain in my love."

"Will you come help your dad clean up the garage?"
"Kids, get your bikes. We're going for a ride!"
"Hey, Honey, I've got some news. We're going to have another baby!"

S trong families have a sense of identity and purpose. They know who they are and why they exist. Whether it's daily chores, dealing with disagreements, helping a family business grow, or building memories on a vacation, every family member knows they are part of something good: their lives are filled with meaning and responsibility. This sense of purpose helps family members work together, make changes for the good of everyone, and welcome the miracle of new family members too.

The final part of the Mass is about identity and purpose. So let's look at the Our Father, the exchange of peace, the reception of Holy Communion, and the dismissal.

Calling God Our Father

"We dare to say, Our Father . . . " Most of us don't feel worthy to call God our Father. On our own, we aren't, but his generous love makes us worthy. In baptism we are born again as sons and daughters of God. In the Lord's Prayer, the word Jesus used for "Father," in Aramaic, is *Abba,* which is a child's intimate term of endearment, more literally, "Daddy" or "Papa." Jesus has gathered us to the Father and invited us, now beloved sons and daughters, to call him Abba.

What do you call God when you pray? Do you think of him as a boss, a landlord, or a kindly but distant grandfather, instead of as your Abba? St. John said, "Beloved, we are God's children now" (1 John 3:2). Do you believe that? Your answer matters, because the question is "What's my identity?" If God is truly your Father, you are truly his beloved child.

A New Kind of Peace

Now we encounter the unique peace of Jesus that is the result of perfect union with God. On the cross, Jesus overcame all that shatters peace: guilt, shame, loss, confusion, doubt, hatred, bitterness, pain, and sin. At Mass, we are invited to share in this new life. Jesus first said, "Peace be with you" to his disciples on the first Easter Sunday, when they'd been hiding behind locked doors in fear (John 20:19). The priest now paraphrases that invitation: *"The peace of the Lord be with you always."*

Outside, the world goes on as it did before, with all that entails—violence, chaos, fear, and death. But inside the room of our hearts, the peace of a new life takes root and flourishes. And by saying, "Peace be with you" to others, we become instruments of the peace of the risen Jesus to our family, friends, and even to perfect strangers.

One with Jesus

The priest now breaks the consecrated host, in preparation for Holy Communion and prays, *"Behold the Lamb of God, behold him who takes away the sins of the world. Blessed are those called to the supper of the Lamb."*

To whom is God sending you?

Why does the liturgy take special care to call Jesus the Lamb of God at this moment in the Mass? There are two important reasons. First, the liturgy recalls the words of John the Baptist, who identified Jesus as the Lamb of God (John 1:29). The second recalls the words of the angel in the Book of Revelation ("Blessed are those who have been called to the wedding feast of the Lamb"—19:9). John's words tell us that communion with Jesus saves us *from* death and evil. The angel's words reveal what communion with Jesus saves us *for*: union with God and a personal sharing in his life.

Neither of these purposes is a private, therapeutic moment with God. The first means a willingness to flee from evil in all its forms; it's a sort of prison break. The second means a willingness to be fruitful, to share your oneness with God with other people. Both understandings require a willingness to move.

On the Move

Next we respond to the priest's declaration that the Lamb of God is here: *"Lord, I am not worthy that you should enter under my roof, but only say the word and my soul shall be healed."* For the first time since Mass began, we move forward, walking toward the Lord, to receive him in Holy Communion. The God we worship becomes our food and drink!

When you return to your pew, do whatever helps you focus on whom (not what!) you've just received. Some people think of Jesus as being present in a thousand different places in the church building, but it's more accurate to hold that a thousand people are made newly present to Jesus. The silence after Holy Communion is meant to be a silence imbued with the inconceivable goodness of our individual and collective intimacy with God and the whole Church. The silence is also a preparation for mission.

Sent with a Purpose

Throughout the Bible, whenever God revealed himself, that revelation led to a divinely assigned task. In the concluding rites of the Mass, we, too, are being commissioned. No one who encounters Christ remains unchanged. God's purpose becomes our purpose. How do we take what he's given us—what he's made us—into the world?

The priest's final words (*"Go and announce the Gospel of the Lord"* or one of the other options) echo Jesus' words when he healed a man and sent him on mission back to his family (Luke 8:39). They echo Mary's actions when she brought the unborn Jesus to her kinswoman Elizabeth. They recall Paul, who brought Jesus to the Gentiles.

To whom is God sending you? At the end of Mass, pray for that person. And then let Jesus launch you on a mission of faith, to share in the work of God.

Does that seem daunting? It is! But the whole Mass is designed to help you see you're not alone. The mission of Jesus can continue only through ongoing closeness to him. Just as Jesus remains in the Father's love—especially as he embraced his cross—so you are empowered to remain with Jesus as you walk out the doors of the church, no matter what challenges you will face.

"Thanks be to God." The final words of the Mass are yours to speak. They are words of gratitude for the mission the Lord has offered you. Why gratitude? Because Jesus will never ask you to do something and then abandon you. As he said the night he gave us the Mass, the secret to bearing fruit as his disciple is to remain with him, like a branch on the vine (John 15:1-5). Without him, you can do nothing. But with him? Nothing is impossible (see Luke 1:37; Philippians 4:13).

Go, and live the intriguing drama of faith. Abandon yourself to the amazing commitment that is life in Christ.

Go and announce the Gospel of the Lord. You are not alone. Thanks be to God!

Questions for Reflection and Discussion

1. When you pray, what do you call God? Do you think of God as a strict father or as Abba?

2. What is your experience of offering the Sign of Peace at Mass? Has this session reinforced or changed how you see the meaning of this moment?

3. Do you remember your first Holy Communion? What did it mean to you then, and what does it mean to you now? How would you describe the link between Holy Communion and a deeper identity as a beloved son or daughter of God?

4. In the Eucharist, we see Jesus as the true Lamb of God. From what attitudes or spiritual dangers do you need the Lamb of God to deliver you? What might be keeping you from consciously bringing these requests to your next Mass?

5. When the priest "dismisses" you or launches you on mission, who comes to your mind? Can you name one person? Several? Your own family members? What are some concrete ways you can better bring the good news of Jesus to them?

At Mass this week, in the silent moments before the final blessing, ask yourself, "What have I received in this Mass? A challenge? An insight? Some wisdom? How has God touched my heart with deeper faith, hope, or love? What habits or behaviors do I want to change or develop? What desires in my heart are stronger because of this Mass?"

If you are moved to do so, jot down your answers to these questions, on paper or in your phone. They are the gifts you take with you on your mission. There's a whole world out there that needs what you've received and what you've become!